EVERYDAY WISDOM
FOR
SUCCESS

More Books by Dr. Wayne W. Dyer

All of the above are available at your
local bookstore, or may be ordered by visiting:

Hay House USA: **www.hayhouse.com**®
Hay House Australia: **www.hayhouse.com.au**
Hay House UK: **www.hayhouse.co.uk**
Hay House India: **www.hayhouse.co.in**

EVERYDAY WISDOM
FOR
SUCCESS

Dr. Wayne W. Dyer

HAY HOUSE, INC.
Carlsbad, California • New York City
London • Sydney • New Dehli

Published in the United States by: Hay House, Inc.: www.hayhouse.com® • *Published in Australia by:* Hay House Australia Pty. Ltd.: www.hayhouse.com.au • *Published in the United Kingdom by:* Hay House UK, Ltd.: www.hayhouse.co.uk • *Published in India by:* Hay House Publishers India: www.hayhouse.co.in

Editorial supervision: Jill Kramer   *Design:* Amy Rose Grigoriou

(Some of the material in this book was excerpted from Wayne Dyer's card decks *Inspiration, The Power of Intention, Inner Peace, 10 Secrets for Success and Inner Peace;* and his books *Being in Balance, Staying on the Path,* and *Everyday Wisdom.*)

Library of Congress Control Number: 2005935415

ISBN 13: 978-1-4019-0552-1

26 25 24 23 22 21 20 19 18 17
1st printing, April 2006

Printed in the United States of America

SUSTAINABLE
FORESTRY
INITIATIVE

Certified Chain of Custody
Promoting Sustainable Forestry

www.sfiprogram.org
SFI-01268

SFI label applies to the text stock

For my son Shane.
I watch you live these principles
every day, and I am so proud.
I love you.

Chasing success is like trying to

squeeze a handful of water.

The tighter you squeeze, the less water

you get. When you chase it, your life

becomes the chase, and you become

a victim of always wanting more.

If you refuse to change your job
(if you don't like it), the only sensible
thing you can do is practice
loving it every day.

Enjoy

everything that happens in

your life, but never make your

happiness or success dependent on

an attachment to any person,

place, or thing.

By referring to previous struggles
and using them as reasons for
not getting on with your life today,
you're assigning responsibility
to the past for why you can't be
successful or happy in the present.

The more you see yourself
as what you'd like to become,
and act as if what you
want is already there,
the more you'll activate
those dormant forces that
will collaborate to transform
your dream into your reality.

When you become certain
that nothing is impossible
for you, you'll attain
everything you desire.

As you engage
in your daily activities,
it's fine to do what you want,
as long as you're not
interfering with anyone
else's right to do the same.

Failure is a judgment, an opinion.

It stems from your fears, which can be

eliminated by love—love for yourself,

love for what you do, love for others,

and love for your planet.

Go the
extra mile
to acquire
what you want
to both attract
and give away.

Know that success
and inner peace
are your birthright;
that you are a child of God;
and as such, that you're
entitled to a life filled with
joy, love, and happiness.

You can't go

around being what everyone

expects you to be, living your

life through other people's rules,

and be happy and successful.

Give thanks for everything that you are and everything that you have—that's the first step toward discarding a scarcity mentality.

As you place more and
more of your energy on
what you intend to manifest,
you'll start seeing those
intentions materializing.

Send out love and harmony, put your mind and body in a peaceful place, and then allow the Universe to work in the perfect way that it knows how.

Each experience in your life was

absolutely necessary in order to have

gotten you to the next place, and

the next, up until this very moment.

Don't equate your self-worth

with how well you do things in life.

You aren't what you *do*.

If you are what you do, then

when you don't . . . you aren't.

Most people are
searching for happiness
outside of themselves. That's
a fundamental mistake.
Happiness is something
you *are*, and it comes from
the way you think.

Never forget that doing what you love is the cornerstone of having success in your life.

You can reshape your thinking so

that you never have to think in

negatives again. You and only

you choose your thoughts.

When you acquire enough inner

peace and feel really positive about

yourself, it's almost impossible for

you to be controlled and manipulated

by anybody else.

You control your emotions. You do not have to explode with anger whenever someone else decides to behave in an angry or vindictive way.

When you become immobilized

by what anybody else thinks of you,

what you're saying is: "Your opinion

of me is more important than

my own opinion of myself."

No one can create negativity
or stress within you. Only *you*
can do that by virtue of how
you process your world.

Either you have control or you don't. If you do, take control; if you don't, don't waste your energy on worry.

You can sit there forever, lamenting

about how bad you've been, feeling

guilty until you die, and not one tiny

slice of that guilt will do anything to

change anything in the past.

One of the highest places
you can get to is to be
independent of the good
opinions of other people.

If you are suffering in your life

right now, I can guarantee that this

condition is tied up with some kind

of attachment to how things

should be going.

When you argue for your
limitations, all you get
are your limitations.

No-limit people are so in charge

that they can trust their instincts,

be childlike, be creative, and do

anything that makes sense to them.

You are in a partnership
with all other human beings,
not a contest to be judged
better than some and
worse than others.

Forgiveness

is the most powerful thing you can

do for yourself. If you can't learn

to forgive, you can forget about

achieving true success

in your life.

Being relaxed, at peace
with yourself, confident,
emotionally neutral, loose, and
free-floating—these are the
keys to successful performance
in almost everything you do.

You're always a valuable, worthwhile human being—not because anybody else says so, not because you're making lots of money—but because you decide to *know* it.

The more you extend kindness to
yourself, the more it will become your
automatic response to others.

Did you ever notice how difficult it is to argue with someone who's not obsessed with being right?

Your soul—that inner quiet
space—is yours to consult.
It will always guide you
in the right direction.

Once you believe in yourself and see

your soul as Divine and precious, you

will automatically become a being

who can create success.

No one can depress you.

No one can make you anxious.

No one can hurt your feelings.

No one can make you anything

other than what you

allow inside.

Be consistently aware of the need

to serve God and serve others

in any and all of your actions.

Having a plan for success

isn't necessarily unhealthy, but

falling in love with the plan is a

real neurosis. . . . Don't let your

plan become bigger than you are.

You have a God-given right to be successful. In your Creator's eyes, no one on this planet is any better than you.

Throughout life,
the two most futile emotions
are guilt for what *has* been
done, and worry about
what *might* be done.

Why not think about some things

you've never done before and do them

simply because you've never done

them and for no other reason?

A sense of purpose is not something that you find; it's something that you are. Truth is not something that you look for; it's something that you live.

You create your thoughts,
your thoughts create your
intentions, and your intentions
create your reality.

The person looking back
at you in the mirror is the
one you have to answer
to every day.

Stop focusing
on what you do not have,
and take stock of all
that you *do* have.

The state of your life is nothing more than a reflection of your state of mind.

If you want to find deeper meaning

in your life, you can't find it in

the opinions or the beliefs that have

been handed to you. You have to go

to that place within yourself.

Anything that bothers you
is only a problem within.
Only *you* can experience it,
and only *you* can correct it.

You have a powerful mind that can

make anything happen as long as

you keep yourself centered.

There is no stress
in the world,
only people
thinking stressful
thoughts.

Life is never boring,

but some people choose

to be bored . . .

boredom is a choice.

If you want to be confident but don't

normally act that way, then today,

just this once, act in the physical

world the way you believe a

confident person would.

Try to learn from the past,
rather than repeating it
and making references
to it all the time.

You can never please everyone.

In fact, if you please 50 percent of

the people, you're doing quite well.

Remember that every single
thing you've gone through
has helped lead you to
where you are today.

You'll come to find that anything you *must* have comes to own you. The funny thing is, when you release it, you start getting more of it.

If you want to find your true

purpose in life, know this for certain:

Your purpose will only be found

in service to others, and in being

connected to something far greater

than your body/mind/ego.

Don't allow the approval and

attention of others to destroy you.

Remain humble and grateful for all of

your accomplishments, and know that

a force greater than your ego is always

at work in your life.

Make an internal
commitment to respect
yourself and feel worthy of all
that the Universe has to offer.

Treat yourself and others with

kindness when you eat, exercise,

play, work, love, and everything else.

In order to get what you want,
monitor your inner dialogue
and match your thoughts to
what you intend to create.

The truth is,
if one of us succeeds,
we all do.

That which offends you only weakens you. Being offended creates the same destructive energy that offended you in the first place—so transcend your ego and stay in peace.

The elevator to success is
out of order today. You're
going to have to take the
stairway, one step at a time.

Let go of your ego's

need to be right. When you're

in the middle of an argument,

ask yourself: *Do I want to*

be right or be happy?

Be thankful for the wonderful gift of being able to serve humanity, your planet, and your God. That's a lot to be grateful for!

No one is capable

of making you upset without your

consent, so if you begin practicing the

intention to be authentic and peaceful

with *everyone*, you connect

to peace itself.

If you get pushed around,
you've been sending
push-me-around signals.

A purpose is not something

that you're going to find.

It's something that will find you.

And it will find you only when

you're ready and not before.

This magnificent Universe provides

abundantly when you're in a

state of gratitude.

Act *as if* what you intend
to manifest in life is already
a reality. Eliminate thoughts
of conditions, limitations, or
the possibility of something
not manifesting.

Determine what you believe
is impossible, and then change
your beliefs.

Genuinely feeling abundant
and successful is possible when
you detach yourself from the
things you desire and allow
them to flow to you—
and *through* you.

All of the "stuff" in your life has arrived to serve you, rather than to make you a servant of the stuff.

You can't expect to draw people

into your life who are kind, confident,

and generous if you're thinking

and acting in cruel, weak, and

selfish ways. You must put forth

what you want to attract.

Know that everything will happen at just the right time, at just the right place, with just the right people.

The qualities of creativity and genius are within you, awaiting your decision to match up with the power of intention.

Every thought that you have impacts you. By shifting in the middle of a weakening thought to one that strengthens, you raise your energy vibration and strengthen yourself and the immediate energy field.

Some people believe that

they live a life of lack because

they're unlucky, instead of realizing

that their belief systems are rooted

in scarcity thinking.

You cannot always be number one,

win a contest, get the merit badge,

or make the honor roll, but you

can always think of yourself as an

important, worthwhile person.

Self-esteem comes from
the self, not from acquisitions
and approval.

It's not what is available or

unavailable that determines your level

of success and happiness; it's what

you convince yourself is true.

Keep a solid picture of the task you want to accomplish in your mind, and refuse to let that intention disappear.

Truly commit to doing
what you love and
loving what you do—today!

Alcohol, as well as all drugs—
legal and otherwise—lower
your body's energy level and
weaken you. By retreating
from these substances,
you can achieve the level
of success you crave.

Just slow down and enjoy it all.

Anonymously perform acts of kindness, expecting nothing in return, not even a thank-you. The universal all-creating Spirit responds to acts of kindness by asking: *How may I be kind to you?*

Your belief about yourself is the most

telling factor in determining your level

of success and happiness.

What you think about expands. If your thoughts are centered on what you're not getting in your life, then what you're not getting, by definition, will have to expand.

Every single condition in
your life can be improved if
you learn to be more effective
at visualizing what you want
and having the intention
to manifest it.

Individuals who use self-labels

are stating, "I'm a finished product

in this area, and I'm never going to

be any different." If you're a finished

product, all tied up and put away,

you've stopped growing.

If you find yourself believing that

you must always be the way you've

always been, you're arguing against

your own personal growth.

To achieve success in all areas, shift your consciousness to an appreciation for all you are and all that you're blessed to have.

Fear of failure becomes fear
of success for those who never
try anything new.

If a problem arises,

then go within.

Get very quiet about it,

and find the answers inside you.

Be cognizant of the fact that the

more you attach your value and

humanity to those things outside

yourself, the more you give those

things the power to control you.

Look upon
every experience you've
ever had, and everyone who's
ever played any role in your
life, as having been sent
to you for your benefit.
In this Universe, there are
simply no accidents.

Money—like health, love, happiness, and all forms of success that you want to create for yourself—is the result of living purposefully. It is not a goal unto itself.

You can never fail in anything
you try to do. You can only
produce certain results.

Involve yourself in
high-energy levels of trust,
optimism, appreciation,
reverence, joy, and love when
you engage in every activity
in your life.

Once you begin working on

your problem areas with small,

daily, success-oriented goals,

the problems will disappear.

If you find yourself being treated in a way you resent or that turns you into a victim, ask yourself this question: "What have I done to teach this person that this behavior is something I'm willing to tolerate?"

The use of mental imagery is one

of the strongest and most effective

strategies for making something

happen for you.

Doing what you love is
the cornerstone of having
abundance in your life.

Take some time to be silent
and repeat the sound of God
as an inner mantra. Meditation
allows you to make conscious
contact with your Source and
achieve success in every area.

Radiate an energy of serenity and

peace so that you have an uplifting

effect on those you come into contact

with. Your presence will make others

feel calm and assured.

You're not what you have
and you're not what you do;
you're an infinite, Divine
being disguised as a successful
person who has accumulated a
certain amount of stuff.
The stuff is not you.

A successful person isn't someone who makes a lot of money. A successful person brings success to everything that he or she does, and money is one of the payoffs.

Have you thought about the fact

that you are the sum total of all your

choices up until this moment?

Happiness and success
are inner processes that we
bring to life's undertakings,
rather than something we
get from "out there."

If you're experiencing scarcity, anguish, depression, an absence of love—or any inability to attract what you desire—seriously look at how you've been drawing these circumstances into your life.

Think about this. If you're still following a career path that you decided upon as a young person, ask yourself this question today: *Would I seek out the advice of a teenager for vocational guidance?*

In business or your personal life, the

more you try to force something for

your own benefit, the less you'll enjoy

what you're seeking so desperately.

The path to the big picture is different

for everyone, but the understanding

has to be that the big picture is,

in fact, *there*.

If there's a pattern of seeing others as failures, you need to notice this pattern as evidence of what *you're* attracting into your life.

There are some people who live 70 years, and there are some people who live one year 70 times, repeating what they're doing over and over in the name of the gold watch or whatever.

Release your need to
feel superior by seeing the
unfolding of Spirit in everyone.
Don't assess others on the
basis of their appearance,
achievements, and possessions.
Remember: *We are all equal
in the eyes of God.*

Choose to be in close proximity to people who are empowering, who see the greatness in you, who feel connected to God, and who live a life that gives evidence that Spirit has found celebration through them.

Successful people learn to *think from the end*—that is, they experience what they wish to intend before it shows up in material form.

You can do the same thing.

Remember this maxim:
*When you change the way
you look at things, the things
you look at change.*
The way you perceive things
is an extremely powerful tool
that will allow you to attain
everything you desire.

There is no *path* to success;

success is an inner attitude that you

bring to your endeavors.

Know that all the abundance
you want is already here. You
just have to tune it in.

Even if you don't know what you

should be doing or what your mission

is, you need to practice creating

that vision anyway.

If you don't have confidence in

yourself, get off your rear end and

do anything that will make you feel

better about yourself.

If you practice
maintaining your composure,
and remember that someone
else's behavior belongs to that
person and cannot upset you
unless you allow it to do so,
then you will not become
an unwilling target.

The opposite of courage

is not so much fear

as it is conformity.

Why not look at your entire life as the unfolding of a plan you participated in before you arrived here? By doing so, you'll shift from blaming others and circumstances to being responsible and feeling your purpose.

Attracting prosperity is just like attracting anything else in your life: It involves not being attached to it, and not giving it power over your life in any way.

On your daily journeys, listen to

those inner signals that help you

make the right choices—no matter

what anyone thinks.

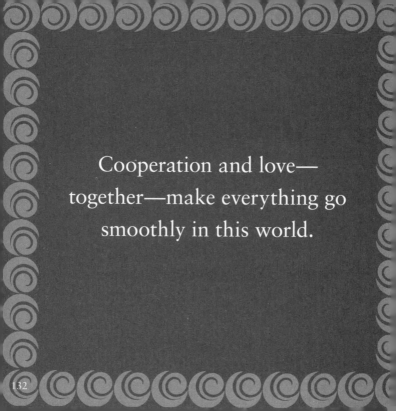

Cooperation and love—together—make everything go smoothly in this world.

Regardless of your current station in life, you have a spiritual contract to make joy your constant companion. Know that you don't have to live a life filled with less-than-joyful activities.

If you slip, it doesn't mean that you're less valuable. It simply means you have something to learn from slipping.

Highly functioning people say,

"Where I am is fine, but I can grow."

Believe that you can attain
anything you wish, and that
you will receive all the help
you need as long as you stay
focused on your goal.

Take stock
of those who were
negative forces in
your past, and search
for ways in which their
actions might have been
blessings in disguise.

Even if you're in the gutter,

you have the option of looking

at the stars.

As you practice speaking
from your truth without
being hurtful or arrogant
in any way, you reconnect with
the energy you emanated
from in the first place.

If you're going to make a difference

in the world, you'll soon learn that

you can't follow the herd.

Try viewing everyone
who comes into your life
as a teacher.

You need to go beyond the
ideas of succeeding and failing,
for these are judgments.
Stay in the process and allow
the Universe to handle
the details.

If you've been

addicted to a harmful substance,

to overeating, or even to being

a doormat, listen to the voice within

that begs you to be big rather

than small, and to take

one corrective step.

If you play the game of life, know that you'll have plenty of wins and losses, regardless of your talent level.

Networking can never fail. It's so powerful because you just keep creating more power sources. It's like geometric progression.

Have faith that God won't send you anything you're incapable of handling. You can decide that the word *fear* is an acronym for false evidence appearing real!

Constantly remind

yourself that you're here

for a reason, and it's not to hoard

a lot of material stuff.

When you're at peace with your

life and in a state of tranquility, you

actually send out a vibration of energy

that impacts all living creatures,

including plants, animals,

and even babies!

Before speaking,
remember that people really do
respect those who are willing
to speak their truth . . . and
even more, to *live* the truth
they feel.

If you find yourself in a difficult job

situation, modify your attitude and

perspective . . . and see how things

change for the better.

Every single person who's drifted in and out of your life is a part of your Divinely chosen experience. So, give thanks for all of these people, and take serious note of what they brought you.

Change your expectations for yourself: Expect the best, expect your fortunes to change, and expect a miracle!

Thinking about where you've been or

what you did wrong in the past are

impediments to a successful life. In an

infinite, never-beginning and never-

ending Universe, there is no past.

Try to free yourself from placing a cash value on everything you have, do, and say. Do what your heart tells you will bring you joy, rather than determining whether it will be cost-effective.

Your limits to success are

defined by the agreement you've made

about what's possible. Change that

agreement and you can dissolve

all these limits.

Self-worth cannot be verified
by others. You're worthy
because you say it is so. If you
depend on others for your
value, it is "other-worth."

Stop blaming your spouse for your unhappiness, your parents for your lack of motivation, the economy for your social status, your childhood for your phobias, and anything else to which you assign blame points. You're the result of the choices *you've* made in your life.

Your ability to be a winner
100 percent of the time is
based upon giving up the
notion that losing at anything
is equivalent to being a loser.

If you're attached to how things

should be going, you're going to find

suffering in your life.

Abundance is about looking at life

and knowing that you have everything

you need for complete happiness, and

then being able to celebrate each and

every moment on Earth.

When you *know* rather than *doubt*, you'll discover the necessary ability to carry out your purpose.

The next time you get nervous about others' opinions, mentally look them in the eye and say, "What you think of me is none of my business."

Did you ever
notice that some people never
have enough, while other
people always do?

The winning attitude is
one that allows you to think
of yourself as a winner all the
time while still giving yourself
room to grow.

Be a student

by staying open

and willing to learn

from everyone

and anyone.

Make cooperation
and service the rule in all your
business dealings.

You go out into the world,
and you are who you choose
to be—and some people will
like it, and others won't.
That's just the way it is.

You have the power to become anything that you want to. Set your expectations for yourself, and know that you'll become whatever you think about.

You are unique in all the world.

You aren't what you do,

so don't equate yourself with your

job or achievements.

Regardless
of how absurd your
inner callings might seem,
they're authentically yours.
The willingness to listen
and act on your inspiration,
independent of the opinions
of others, is imperative.

You'll come to know that
the fear of not *having* enough
prevents many from seeing that
they already *are* enough.

Since the Universe works via the Law of Attraction, when you say, "Gimme, gimme, gimme," it responds in like fashion. But when you ask, "How may I share?" the Universe responds, "How may *I* share with *you*?"

You're only feeling stuck
if you decide to be.
So decide differently.

Make peace with silence, and remind

yourself that it is in this space that

you'll come to remember your spirit.

When you're able to transcend

an aversion to silence, you'll also

transcend many other miseries.

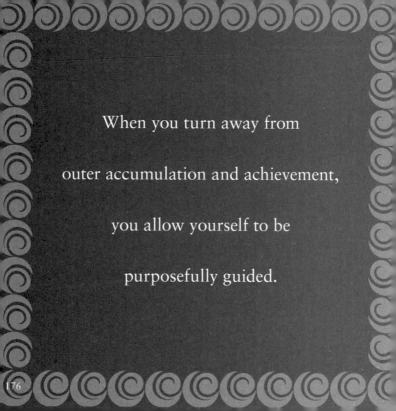

When you turn away from

outer accumulation and achievement,

you allow yourself to be

purposefully guided.

Be on the lookout to see
the God-force everywhere,
in every living thing. Be
cognizant of how this force
has delivered many blessings to
you throughout your life and
continues to do so.

Begin observing your thoughts,
and notice if you're going in
the wrong direction. You can,
with conscious effort, make a
U-turn with new thoughts.

Anything

that keeps you from growing

is never

worth defending.

Your reputation is in the
hands of others. That's what a
reputation is. You can't control
that. The only thing you can
control is your character.

In

virtually every

area of your life,

the more you give away,

the more you get back.

Before beginning your day, spend

some time with God during the early

morning. In these moments, reflect,

feel the peace, and most important,

extend your gratitude.

Choose to associate with
people who are successful.
But first you need to identify
those who are inspired and
inspiring—individuals who've
risen above their egos and the
vanities of the world.

Extend some kind of unexpected

generosity to someone, preferably a

stranger, every single day for

two weeks. The more you practice

being generous, the more

you'll impact others.

Be grateful to all those people
who told you no. It's because
of them that you managed
to do it all yourself.

When an idea's time has come,

it can't be stopped. And the reverse

of this is true: An idea whose time

hasn't come can't be created.

In any
challenging situation,
ask yourself this:
*Am I part of the problem
or part of the
solution?*

As you look back on your life,
know that you've failed
at nothing. Failure can only
be in your mind.

The highest form of ignorance
is to reject something you
know nothing about.

Know that for every act of apparent

evil, there are a million acts of

kindness, and that's where you need

to focus your attention.

Be aware that anything that immobilizes you, gets in your way, or keeps you from your goals is all yours. You can throw it away anytime you choose.

Remind yourself that if you can conceive it in your mind, then it can be brought into your physical world.

If you fail

to align your thoughts with

the success you're capable of

attracting, the weight of the dominant

thoughts will tip the scale away

from a balanced life.

Every moment that you spend upset,

in despair, in anguish, angry, or hurt

because of the behavior of anybody

else in your life is a moment in which

you've given up control of your life.

The two
most unnecessary emotions
in life are
guilt and worry.

Failure

is an editorial

judgment

imposed

by others.

Have you considered that risks are nothing more than thoughts that you've convinced yourself are impossible to implement?

Every thought of frustration is like purchasing a ticket for more frustration. Every thought that agrees that you're stuck is asking the Universe to send you even *more* of that glue to *keep* you stuck.

Commit to thinking about
what you want, rather than
how impossible or difficult a
dream may seem.

If you're obsessed with defeating the other guy and winning at all costs, then you're guaranteed to attract the vibrational equivalent of this thinking into your life—even if you do yoga and stand on your head chanting mantras every day!

Always
remember that every
obstacle is a test *and*
an opportunity.

You need to learn how
to create a match between
what it is that you desire in
your life, and what thoughts,
or vibrational energy, you're
choosing to attract
those desires.

Habits are changed by practicing

new behavior, and this is true for

mental habits as well.

Go on a rampage of appreciation, rather than discussing the evils of the world, and offer joyful commentary whenever possible.

There's no scarcity of opportunity

to make a living at what you love.

There's only a scarcity of resolve

to make it happen.

Make a conscious decision to look for

what is right and pleasing in others.

Decide that you're going to disregard

stereotypes, and refuse to engage

in conversations that dwell on

judging anyone.

If you can imagine

yourself succeeding in some area,

then you can.

Nothing you imagine

in your mind is impossible.

If you feel strongly that you came here for a particular purpose, then you should cultivate energy to match this dream. Your current financial status is unimportant when it comes to your pursuit of this purpose.

You need

to keep reminding yourself that

you are a Divine piece of God.

Feeling as if you're unworthy of God's

abundance is the same as denying

your spiritual essence.

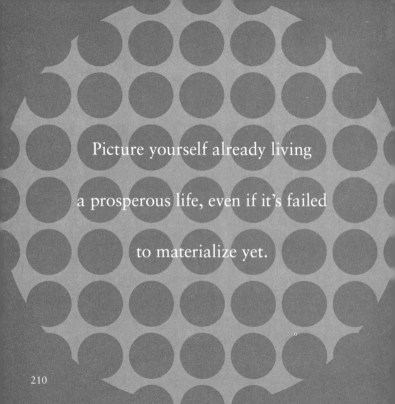

Picture yourself already living

a prosperous life, even if it's failed

to materialize yet.

If your luck appears to be bad,
shift your expectations around.
Make every effort to stay in balance
with what you do desire, rather than
what you've been attracting.

There are limits to material growth, but there are no limits to inner enlightenment.

Know in your heart that you

don't need one more thing to make

yourself complete, and then watch all

those external things become less

and less significant.

Advance confidently in the
direction of your own dreams
to live the life that you've
imagined. That's when
you have success.

Name it,

and if you can dream it,

you can achieve it.

Anything you want
to succeed in,
you can do—*anything!*

About the Author

Affectionately called the "father of motivation" by his fans, **Dr. Wayne W. Dyer** was an internationally renowned author, speaker, and pioneer in the field of self-development. Over the four decades of his career, he wrote more than 40 books (21 of which became *New York Times* bestsellers), created numerous audio programs and videos, and appeared on thousands of television and radio shows. His books *Manifest Your Destiny, Wisdom of the Ages, There's a Spiritual Solution to Every Problem,* and the *New York Times* bestsellers *10 Secrets for Success and Inner*

Peace, The Power of Intention, Inspiration, Change Your Thoughts—Change Your Life, Excuses Begone!, Wishes Fulfilled, and *I Can See Clearly Now* were all featured as National Public Television specials.

Wayne held a doctorate in educational counseling from Wayne State University, had been an associate professor at St. John's University in New York, and honored a lifetime commitment to learning and finding the Higher Self. In 2015, he left his body, returning to Infinite Source to embark on his next adventure.

Website: www.DrWayneDyer.com

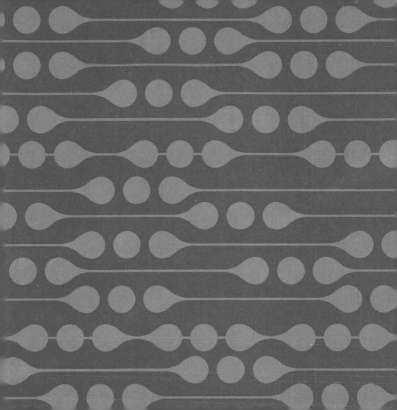

Hay House Titles of Related Interest

Everyday Positive Thinking,
by Louise Hay

The Success Book,
by John Randolph Price

Success Cards,
by Deepak Chopra

Trust Your Vibes at Work,
and Let Them Work for You,
by Sonia Choquette

You Can Live an Amazing Life . . .
in Just 60 Days!
by Dr. John F. Demartini

These books are available
at your local bookstore, or may be ordered by visiting:

Hay House USA: www.hayhouse.com®
Hay House Australia: www.hayhouse.com.au
Hay House UK: www.hayhouse.co.uk
Hay House India: www.hayhouse.co.in

Notes

Notes

Notes

Notes

Notes

Notes